INSIDE SPECIAL FORCES ™

BLACK OPS
AND OTHER SPECIAL MISSIONS OF THE
U.S. AIR FORCE COMBAT CONTROL TEAM

Peter Ryan

rosen publishing's
rosen central

New York

Published in 2013 by The Rosen Publishing Group, Inc.
29 East 21st Street, New York, NY 10010

Copyright © 2013 by The Rosen Publishing Group, Inc.

First Edition

Library of Congress Cataloging-in-Publication Data

Ryan, Peter K.
Black ops and other special missions of the U.S. Air Force combat control team/Peter Ryan.—1st ed.
        p. cm.—(Inside special forces)
Includes bibliographical references and index.
ISBN 978-1-4488-8382-0 (library binding)—
ISBN 978-1-4488-8389-9 (pbk.)—
ISBN 978-1-4488-8392-9 (6-pack)
1. United States. Air Force—Combat controllers—
Juvenile literature. 2. Close air support—Juvenile
literature. 3. Afghan War, 2001—Commando operations—
United States—Juvenile literature. 4. Afghan War, 2001—
Aerial operations, American—Juvenile literature. I. Title.
UG703.R93 2013
358.4—dc23

                                                                      2012022066

Manufactured in the United States of America

CPSIA Compliance Information: Batch #W13YA: For further information, contact Rosen Publishing, New York, New York, at 1-800-237-9932.

CONTENTS

INTRODUCTION

IN OCTOBER 2009, in Herat Province, Afghanistan, a U.S. Army Green Beret team was sent to find a Taliban leader and capture or kill him to reduce the Taliban's effectiveness. The team was sent in at night to improve its chances of a fully covert mission. However, upon entering the suspected village where the target should have been found, there waited an ambush. Rooftop snipers in nested machine gun positions pinned the team down and drew it into a prolonged firefight. Fortunately for the Green Berets they had Staff Sgt. Robert Gutierrez with them, an experienced and capable combat controller. Sgt. Gutierrez was able to call in air support from nearby A-10 Thunderbolt aircraft to deliver close combat strafing runs, delivering deadly damage to the ambushing forces.

In the midst of the battle, Sgt. Gutierrez was shot in the chest, and the bullet passed through his lung. Fortunately, he was accompanied by Army Sergeant 1st Class Michael Jones, a Green Beret medic. Sgt. Jones was able to use a needle decompression on Sgt. Gutierrez's chest to prevent his lung from collapsing. Although badly wounded and in need of repeated chest decompressions, Sgt. Gutierrez never removed his radio headset and kept calling in and guiding repeated air assaults on the nearby enemy position. Sgt. Gutierrez called in an evacuation for himself and other wounded members of the Green

Beret team, and despite his major chest wound, he was able to hike 1 mile (1.6 kilometers) to a safe landing zone for medical extraction by helicopter. Sgt. Gutierrez's actions saved the lives of many of his teammates that night and earned him the U.S. Air

Combat controllers will often undertake missions at night, such as this operation in Afghanistan, to reduce the likelihood of being seen by enemy forces.

Force Cross, the highest honor awarded in the U.S. Air Force, for bravery and exemplary conduct.

Combat controllers are highly trained members of the U.S. Air Force Special Operations Command. Their role is to provide ground-based air traffic control for aircraft landing, air-to-ground assault, and combat air control. Combat controllers are some of the most highly trained special operations personnel in all of the U.S. military. They provide a combination of commando tactical capabilities and aircraft command and control to deliver deadly air attacks across a wide range of needs.

Like all of their special operations comrades, combat controllers are commandos, trained in the art of covert warfare, close combat, parachuting, scuba, demolitions, and special weapons training. However, the skills that set combat controllers apart are their training and certification as air traffic controllers and joint terminal attack controllers. Those two skills earn combat controllers a special role on many special operations teams, where they serve as "force multipliers" able to radically enhance the effectiveness of any team.

Given the increasing technological sophistication of the modern battlefield, combat controllers represent the peak of cross-discipline capability. With their ability to operate alongside U.S. Navy SEALs, Army Green Berets, Marine Force Recon, and Army Rangers, combat controllers are considered some of the most versatile and valuable special operations assets in the entire U.S. armed services.

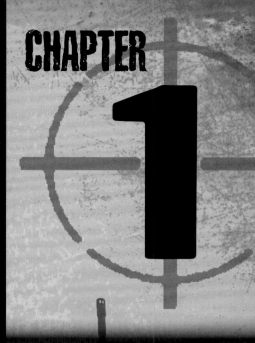

LE

T

LLER

AL OPERATIONS commandos
at Control Team, or combat con-
bers of the Air Force Special
mand. Combat controllers are
any to be among the very best
al operations groups throughout
ned services. They are trained
firearms, counterterrorism,
command, flight traffic control,
ack control, fire support, water-
, parachute-based infiltration,
ended mission deployments. In
ntrollers are trained to be the
e ground in any conditions and at

bles that combat controllers
nly deployed for are providing
ack command for special opera-
or the capture and command of

air bases for use by the U.S. Air Force. The combat controller motto "First There" accurately describes their role; they are the first on the ground to direct the arrival of the supporting forces. Because they are the "First There," they must be the best trained and most capable in order to achieve their mission.

The role of the combat controller has evolved since its inception during World War II. The U.S.

Combat controllers in Afghanistan practice capturing an airfield and managing air traffic control. Airfield capture and command is one of the core missions of the Combat Control Team.

Army was in need of a special commando who could get behind enemy lines, far ahead of any support or extraction, to guide the landing of assault gliders delivering U.S. Army forces to the battle. The very first combat controllers were forged in combat and had very little time to prepare for their role. However, in their first deployment, they dramatically reduced the casualty rates of army gliders and army paratroopers through their efforts.

As air power became the deciding force driving U.S. global military superiority, the role of the combat controller evolved to include air-to-ground attack control. Combat controllers developed tools and skills to use their ground positions to guide air assaults with increased accuracy and effectiveness. This role has continually evolved, and today the combat controllers are highly sought-after assets that all branches of the military seek to deploy to ensure the success and survivability of their missions.

Within the special operations groups throughout the U.S. military there are common skill sets and training to prepare special operations commandos. This training is reserved for the most physically and mentally capable soldiers. Special operators are trained in all forms of hand-to-hand combat, covert maneuvers, water maneuvers, air maneuvers, vehicle utilization, special weapons, and demolitions. A commando is a one-man platoon, able to deliver overwhelming force and capability.

Each branch of the U.S. military has its own special operations groups, each one designed and trained to fulfill a variety of specialized mission types, along with essential commando soldiering. The Navy SEALs are experts at water-based infiltration and covert operations. Marine Force Recon units are long-range ground-based reconnaissance experts. The Green Berets, also called Special Forces, are both commandos and experts at counterterrorism and insurgency. The Army Rangers are all-purpose commandos able to fulfill a variety of combat roles in many theaters. The Air Force combat controllers are unique in their ability to bring aircraft resources to bear as deadly attackers or as transportation.

Unlike any other special operations group, combat controllers are most often deployed into units of special operations groups from other branches of the military. Combat controllers are often deployed with Green Beret, Ranger, or Navy SEAL units in order to provide their invaluable air control capability. Since the

A combat controller coordinates air traffic control for a battlefield runway.

start of the wars in Afghanistan and Iraq in early 2002, the combat controller has become an indispensable asset that all special operations teams seek to add to their teams. The combat controller can bring air-to-ground assaults and air rescue to the special operations teams with more accuracy and greater success than any other special operator, increasing the likelihood of mission success and unit survival.

Combat controllers have a large burden to bear because they have to be able to expertly utilize their air command capability to accurately guide air strikes, landings, and extractions. They also have to be highly effective and lethal commandos able to stand toe-to-toe with any other special operations teams. Combat controllers are rare soldiers who are expert marksmen, incredible athletes, skilled hand-to-hand fighters, and capable survivalists able to work in the field for indefinite periods of time. Combat controllers are part Rambo and part Buzz Aldrin embodied in one combatant.

The reason that combat controllers see so much combat and regular deployment is because they are some of the most valuable soldiers on the battlefield. A single combat controller is able to multiply the offensive strength of any combat team many times over. Navy SEALs, considered to be the best small-arms combatants in the world, cannot deliver the same lethality that a combat controller with a radio and a fighter jet overhead can. A single combat controller can mean the difference between mission success and certain doom. There are few in the armed

THE MODERN SOLDIER

Combat controllers are an example of the rapid evolution of the soldier due to the advancement of communication technologies. One of the best examples of combat controllers' advanced technology capabilities is their ability to interact with drones for the gathering of intelligence and for guided air-to-ground assault.

The Predator drone is the most advanced drone in use today, and the operators of that craft can oftentimes be thousands of miles away from the drone. Combat Control Teams on the ground will communicate with the drone pilot to deliver missiles and bombs in locations where normally piloted aircraft could not venture due to risk and topography.

forces who can deliver lethal small-arms fire in the middle of combat while simultaneously calling in air strikes and evacuations and providing on-the-ground situational awareness to any friendly aircraft.

AIR BASE CAPTURE AND COMMAND

One of the rare times that a team of combat controllers would work together is for the capture and command of an air base. The Combat Control Team (CCT) trains for this scenario as part of its core regimen. They are air traffic controllers, and they are needed

Combat controllers, such as this one practicing patrolling for enemy forces, are experts at ground combat operations and train continuously in simulated exercises.

on the front lines to safely control the air space and guide planes to land in air bases that are very unsafe.

The first part of the capture and command mission, capture, requires the CCT to use stealth and coordination to take the base by whatever means necessary. Because air bases are usually very heavily defended and well behind enemy lines, CCTs must be the very best at ground combat and lethality. CCTs will use stealth, force, surprise, and any other tactic that will get the job done.

One critical element they must always be aware of is the preservation and condition of the runway and the air traffic tower. Once the base has been captured, the CCT will then take control of the runway and use the air traffic tower to begin controlling the overhead airspace to guide aircraft to land on that base. Capture and command of an enemy air base is a specialty of the CCT and one of the reasons why they have earned the motto "First There."

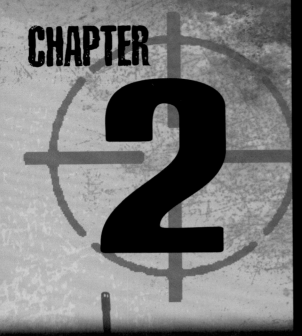

CHAPTER 2

TRAINING

PHYSICAL FITNESS AND MENTAL capability are absolutely critical to the role of the combat controller. The candidate who chooses to pursue a career as a combat controller must endure all forms of harsh environments, extreme physical challenges, and extremely dangerous activity, and must have the mental acuity to guide every manner of aircraft from the ground, despite extreme fatigue and starvation.

PAST

Fewer than 10 percent of candidates who attempt the combat controller training make it past the first round of tests. The test is intentionally rigorous in order to eliminate all but the most physically and mentally capable of candidates. The first requirement that candidates must pass is meeting the PAST, or Physical Ability and Stamina Test.

The PAST requires that candidates meet the following requirements:

- Two 25-meter underwater swims with 3 minutes between trials.
- A 500-meter swim within 11:42 minutes
- A 1.5-mile run within 10:10 minutes
- Eight pull-ups within 2 minutes
- Forty-eight sit-ups within 2 minutes
- Forty-eight push-ups within 2 minutes
- A 3-mile rucksack march (50 lb. load) within 45 minutes.

Physical fitness is a major requirement of excelling in PAST. Calisthenics and endurance exercises are a regular part of the initial and ongoing training of all combat controllers.

Passing the PAST is the minimum requirement for the potential candidate to even be considered. Once this initial hurdle has been met, the candidate must then endure the Combat Control Selection Course at Lackland Air Force Base in Texas, which is two weeks of grueling physical and mental tests to weed out all but the very toughest of candidates. This two-week course includes intense physical training, intense water testing, sleep deprivation, long marches, and many more challenges all designed to test the limits of the candidates. It is expected that most candidates will not pass the selection course.

AFSOC

The Air Force Special Operations Command (AFSOC) contains two major Special Tactics Groups: the 720th based at Hurlburt Air Force Base in Florida and the 724th based at Pope Air Force Base in North Carolina. There are approximately one thousand airmen between the 720th and 724th STGs. Underneath the 720th Group, there are six Special Tactics Squadrons, including CCTs, PJs, SOWTs, TACPs, one Air National Guard team dedicated to augmenting the humanitarian efforts of the 720th, and two internationally based STSs. Underneath the 724th are two STSs; the 724th is the newer STG, formed in 2011, and it is adding more squads each year as a result of the incredible demand for additional combat controllers in the field.

COMBAT CONTROL OPERATOR COURSE

Upon completion of the selection course, successful candidates move on to the Combat Control Operator Course at Keesler Air Force Base in Mississippi. This course is eighty days and split into two phases, Combat Control Fundamentals (twenty-eight days) and Combat Control Apprentice-Tower (fifty-two days). This course is the same one that all U.S. Air Force air traffic controllers undergo, except that combat controllers endure intensive daily physical and combat training. Successfully completing this course and passing the required examinations qualifies the candidate to perform as a certified FAA air traffic controller.

TRAINING SCHOOLS

Following the completion of the combat control course, the candidate moves on to U.S. Army Airborne School at Fort Benning, Georgia. This course is fifteen days and is identical to the course that all Army Airborne soldiers go through. The candidate learns basic parachuting during this course.

After Airborne School, the candidate moves on to U.S. Air Force Basic Survival School at Fairchild Air Force Base, Washington. This course lasts nineteen days and includes wilderness survival and SERE (survival, evasion, resistance, and escape) training to prepare candidates for the challenge of battlefield conditions and being captured by the enemy.

Following Survival School is the Combat Control School at Pope Air Force Base, North Carolina. This course lasts eighty-four days and provides essential commando training for combat zones, along with specialized combat controller skills. This course is the final step of the process before a candidate becomes a combat controller. However, successful completion of this course entitles the now "journeyman" combat controller only to undergo further training before he is fully prepared for combat duty.

The new combat controller moves on to the Special Tactics Advanced Skills Training program at

Combat controllers perform helicopter insertion and extraction exercises at Hurlburt Airfield. Helicopters are used extensively by the combat controllers to insert to the front lines of combat.

Hurlburt Field, Florida. It is a yearlong program that delivers the extensive specialized training that sets combat controllers apart from other special operators. This includes air control training, airfield capture, assault training, and more. This is the stage of training that provides the combat controller with the skills and capabilities that set him apart from other special operators. He becomes a master of ground combat who simultaneously owns the airspace around him.

AFSOC IN JAPAN

Following the massive 8.9 magnitude earthquake and tsunami that devastated Japan in March 2011, AFSOC sent a team of combat controllers along with other members of AFSOC and multiple pieces of equipment to Japan to assist with the reopening of Matsushima and Sendai airports. The teams landed at Matsushima, where they assisted local air traffic control and defense forces to reestablish the airfield to begin the delivery of needed emergency supplies. Part of that CCT broke off and drove to Sendai airport, which was more badly damaged, and began the process of reestablishing that airport for use. The aid of those controllers was critical to the Japanese and international aid agencies delivering personnel and equipment and for the delivery of humanitarian assistance to those regions.

During the yearlong Advanced Skills Training course, the command controller trainees will also attend the U.S. Army Military Free-Fall Parachutist School at Fort Bragg, North Carolina, and Yuma, Arizona. Trainees will learn high-altitude parachuting techniques and perform multiple jumps through the course.

Trainees will also attend the U.S. Air Force Combat Divers School at Panama City, Florida, where they will learn advanced scuba (self-contained underwater breathing apparatus) and ccuba (closed-circuit

HALO jumps allow combat controllers to reach their mission points stealthily and quickly. Combat controllers are expert high-altitude parachutists.

underwater breathing apparatus) combat techniques to prepare to operate alongside any other water-based special operations teams.

From start to finish, the total training time that a combat controller undergoes is nearly two years. At the completion of the full training cycle, the combat controller has further continued-training options, including the Joint Tactical Attack Command qualification, which every combat controller achieves, and other specialized training provided by multiple training schools across the U.S. military.

Fully trained, a combat controller is able to jump from a plane, emerge from a submarine, drive across land in a variety of ground vehicles, deploy and disarm demolitions, engage in ground combat, provide extended reconnaissance, and provide air command and control using handheld communications equipment from anywhere in the world.

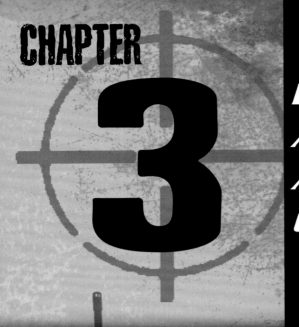

CHAPTER 3

EQUIPMENT AND VEHICLES, AIRCRAFT, AND CAPABILITIES

THE MOST IMPORTANT TOOL in the combat controller's arsenal is his radio and his Battlefield Air Operations (BAO) kit. With those two pieces of equipment alone, a combat controller is able to command all variety of aircraft across all branches of the U.S. military. The combat controller will carry two identical radios. If one of the radios is damaged the other is available.

Other standard equipment that combat controllers use are the Battlefield Airman Operational kit, a combination vest, a pack, and integrated computer and radio equipment. The BAO kit is an operational command system (OCS) that combat controllers will use to interface with the Joint Terminal Attack Controller (JTAC), an information network that provides battlefield and air awareness across a wide array of users.

Combat controllers enter the battlefield with both scuba gear and their BAO kits. Amphibious assault is one of the many methods CCTs use to achieve their missions.

The BAO kit is the integrated system that allows the combat controller to coordinate with aircraft and other intelligence assets through the JTAC. The combat controller will be able to deliver detailed information about weather, enemy positions, ground formations, equipment movement, and many other vital pieces of information that enable pilots to more accurately perform their job. Additionally, with the JTAC network the combat controller is able to more accurately communicate both landing and attack coordinates to pilots to enhance mission success rates.

GEAR

In addition to telecommunication equipment, combat controllers carry a wide variety of gear and weaponry. Combat controllers are well trained in marksmanship and combat fire, and they are armed with an assault rifle, a pistol, grenades, demolitions equipment, antitank launchers, and other deadly weapons. Combat controllers enter the field with their tactical harnesses and rucksacks loaded with upward of 60 pounds (27.2 kilograms) of equipment, not including their weaponry.

Most combat controllers wear plate body armor, which adds greatly to the weight of the soldiers' gear, during ground maneuvers to protect their major organs, extremities, and head. Parachute equipment is also standardized so that any member of a team can safely identify and use the equipment and can support fellow combatants during a jump. Standard underwater gear is also utilized, including both scuba (self-contained underwater breathing apparatus) and ccuba (closed-circuit underwater breathing apparatus) systems; ccuba systems are closed loops, and the diver rebreathes his own air with oxygen added in, preventing any discharge of bubbles, which can be seen and heard on the surface. These systems are used when stealth is required.

WEAPONRY

Currently the assault rifles that combat controllers use are the M-4 rifle and the newer Mark 17 SCAR-H. The most recently approved pistol used in the CCT is the Glock 19 9mm. Combat controllers, like all other special operations groups, have more freedom and flexibility to choose their weaponry and gear in order to meet the operational requirements of their missions. Consequently, special operators are often chosen to test new equipment for evaluation by the military for wider adoption.

Grenades and grenade launchers are standard weapons of choice for combat controllers, and the new SCAR-H has a modular 203mm grenade launcher

A combat controller practices firing his M-4 carbine, shown here with optional under-mounted M-203 grenade launcher.

that can be carried into the field and attached to the rifle with relative ease. The CCT is one of the pilot testing teams vetting the SCAR-H and its various attachments for field use across the military. The SCAR-H represents the future of the assault rifle in the U.S. military: lightweight, modular, durable, and highly accurate, with a large bore round.

VEHICLES

In some conditions, combat controllers will require the use of special operations assault and transportation vehicles. Controllers are trained in the operation and battlefield maintenance of ATV equipment and certain special operations high-speed attack vehicles.

Other vehicles that combat controllers are trained to interact with as passengers or controllers are the PAVE Low helicopter, AC-130 gunship, EC-130SJ Talon and EC-130 E/H Super

The CV-22 Osprey (top) is a large, fast transport that will deliver combat controllers to the field. The Raven UAV allows controllers to remotely observe forward positions.

Talon special operations transport planes, and CV-22 Osprey pivot wing aircraft. Combat controllers regularly practice boarding and exiting different vehicle and aircraft models in training drills in order to be

THE ORIGIN OF THE COMBAT CONTROL TEAM

During World War II, the Air Force was a part of the U.S. Army. World War II was the first war in which the U.S. Army used airplanes to deliver large troop divisions to combat zones. This large-scale air delivery required a major coordination effort to guide the aircraft to the proper landing zone and to safely pilot and land the aircraft.

In order to achieve this, the U.S. Army used its elite Pathfinder teams, who were the predecessors of today's Army Rangers. The Pathfinder teams were not properly trained in air command, and many botched missions saw aircraft landing off target, sadly causing many fatalities. In response to this, a new small team was formed, called the Combat Control Team, tasked specifically with guiding troop-carrying gliders. They received intense special training in air traffic control, weather analysis and forecasting, communications, cryptography, and signaling. On their first mission, Operation Varsity, the new Combat Control Teams successfully guided four Airborne divisions to their designated drop zones with minimal loss. Their work was considered a huge success, and their place in the U.S. Army Air Force was cemented.

prepared to jump, rappel, parachute, or evacuate at a moment's notice. Combat controllers learn as much as they can about the vehicles they interact with so that in a combat or high-stress situation they are prepared to rapidly adapt and act without hesitation.

Very recently, combat controllers have begun to make use of unmanned aerial vehicles (UAVs), also known as drones. Combat controllers are trained to carry small, lightweight surveillance drones with them into the field for use as intelligence-gathering tools. The WASP III and the RQ-11B Raven can be carried by a single controller and launched by hand to provide the operator with the ability to gather intelligence about forward enemy positions, landscape, and topography. Drones take away a lot of the risk of physical reconnaissance and provide the operator with the chance to scout an area before moving into it.

DEPLOYMENT SCENARIOS

Although the combat controller is part of the Combat Control Team and part of the larger 720th Special Tactics Squadron of the Air Force Special Operations Command, combat controllers are most often deployed into teams from other branches of the military.

The most common deployment that a controller will be assigned is with either a Green Beret or Navy SEAL unit. The reason is the controller's ability to augment both units' air superiority posture and air-based evacuation potential. In standard fire-based combat, a Green Beret or Navy SEAL team is almost unrivaled by any other team in the world. However, when a situation develops in which the unit is vastly outnumbered or pinned down by tanks or distant artillery, having a combat controller on the team to call in precision strikes on enemy targets is invaluable.

Prior to 2001, combat controllers were not wanted in other special operations teams. There was a belief that combat controllers were unable to keep up with other special operations teams and that having them

The Special Weathermen team, another unit in the AFSOC, uses weather balloons to gather valuable weather data for use in formulating large-scale combat plans. Controllers and weathermen teams occasionally train and operate together.

around would only endanger the team. However, the Afghanistan and Iraq wars proved very quickly that special operations teams could be substantially improved by the addition of combat controllers. Famous battles in Afghanistan proved that combat controllers were not only skillful at bringing air strikes to the battle but were also as tough as nails. By 2012, there were few special operations teams that would head into the field without taking a combat controller with them. The demand for controllers has grown so fast that there is a new effort to enhance the number of them in the training pipeline.

There are circumstances when a team of controllers, a true Combat Control Team, will operate as a deployed unit. The most common reason for a CCT unit deployment is for an airfield incursion and seizure. The CCT will storm an air base, pacify any resistance, capture the command facilities, take over the air traffic control tower, and use the air base for the landing of U.S. Air Force planes. Air base capture is one of the core missions that combat controllers train for as individuals and as a team.

There are other circumstances when a controller may team with some of the other members of the 720th Special Tactics Squadron, the Pararescue Jumpers, the Special Operations Weathermen, or the Tactical Air Command Party. These four teams are all special operations forces within the AFSOC, and they all have unique roles. In unison they represent a very capable force able to accomplish unique tactical and strategic objectives.

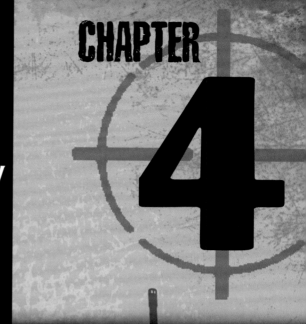

NOVEMBER 16, 2001: TARIN KOWT, AFGHANISTAN

CHAPTER 4

THE BATTLE FOR TARIN KOWT

DURING THE FIRST DAYS of the U.S. invasion of Afghanistan, combat controllers were among the very first special operations forces on the ground. Afghanistan is a very mountainous country, and one that has been at war with one nation or another since the 1980s. The Taliban had very securely hidden cave complexes in the mountains that provided excellent protection from both ground and air forces.

A mixed team of Army Green Berets, CIA special operators, tribal Afghan resistance fighters, and a combat controller were on a special mission led by Afghan Hamid Karzai to capture the city of Tarin Kowt, the capitol of Uruzgan Province. The team captured the city and dug in to defend against an approaching enemy force

31

of vastly superior numbers with heavy weaponry and vehicles. The team commander, in coordination with his assigned combat controller, called in wave after wave of air-to-ground assaults, completely decimating the opposing Taliban force. Without the assigned combat controller, the unit would likely have sustained heavy casualties, possibly including Karzai, who is now the president of Afghanistan.

Tarin Kowt is a very isolated and mountainous region. It has important strategic value because of its proximity to the southern provinces it borders.

The victory was so decisive that Tarin Kowt is considered to be the turning point that began the demise of the Taliban. The combat controller used his radio and JTAC equipment to call in air strikes from A-10 Thunderbolts and AC-130 gunships. The Taliban had not encountered enemy resistance of this nature before. The intensity of the firepower brought to bear by the combat controller was overwhelmingly lethal and incredibly precise. The presence of the combat controller in this team made the difference between success and failure for this joint operation team. The message that it sent to the Taliban resistance was that the forces the United States could bring to the fight were more formidable than previously assumed.

A-10s are twin-engine planes designed to fly into combat at low altitude and high speeds to attack tanks and other ground units. A-10s have very thick outer hulls and are able to take direct hits from small arms fire (rifles, machine guns) with almost no loss of capability. A-10s carry both missiles and bombs and are fitted with spinning barrel Vulcan machine cannons capable of firing thousands of rounds of large projectiles in only a few seconds.

AC-130s are larger aircraft that fly several thousand feet above the combat zone in a circular pattern around the battlefield. Ground-based controllers provide detailed firing coordinates, and the AC-130 crew will unleash devastating firepower from a 25mm, 40mm, or 105mm cannon. Each cannon is used for distinct target types: the 25mm is for antipersonnel, and the 40mm is for antipersonnel, light vehicles, and light defensive positions. The 105mm is a devastating cannon that can destroy tanks, buildings, bunkers, and other defensive positions. The precision guidance of the ground-based combat controller makes the AC-130 one of the most lethal tools in the CCT arsenal.

Though highly skilled and well-trained airmen fly the A-10 and the AC-130, their ability to accurately deliver munitions to their target is fully dependent

The AC-130U aircraft is regularly called in by combat controllers to conduct air strikes.

upon the on-the-ground guidance of a JTAC operator. The training that combat controllers receive prepares them to employ precise targeting methods for the delivery of fire from many types of attack craft. The A-10 attack pattern requires the combat controller to view the battlefield from a low-altitude perspective, while the attack pattern of the AC-130 requires the combat controller to view the battlefield from a high-altitude perspective. Additional kinds of air attacks can be called in that require substantially different calculations and guidance.

Combat controllers are trained to keep their calm under pressure and are able to monitor their surroundings, their teammates, and the enemy to

ROYAL CANADIAN AIR FORCE 427TH SPECIAL OPERATIONS AVIATION SQUADRON

The Royal Canadian Air Force 427th Special Operations Aviation Squadron is the Canadian equivalent of the U.S. Air Force Special Operations Command. It is a squadron of elite pilots and aircrews who fly special operations missions around the world. Although the 427th does not have a dedicated tactical commando squadron, it does work extensively with the Canadian Forward Air Controllers (FAC). FACs perform similarly to the CCT, providing ground-based air traffic control, airfield control, and tactical air-to-ground attack control. The 427th is undergoing realignment so it is very feasible that the Canadians will develop their own dedicated equivalent to the CCT.

provide accurate information to aircraft at all times. As the situation on the ground changes, the combat controllers must adapt their efforts and call varying types of air attacks to adjust to the changes. A fast attack from an A-10 may not be effective when the enemy is hidden in a bunker, so it may require the controller to call in a precision bomb drop from an F-15. When wind patterns change, the controller must account for their effect on the path of flight of munitions and the potential impact on the aircraft being called in. When fog or other inclement weather makes visibility from the air impossible, the controller must be able to guide the pilot to deliver attacks using only his instrumentation.

THE SIEGE OF TORA BORA

The mountainous region known as Tora Bora was a stronghold of the Taliban. Mountain cave networks formed a well-fortified stronghold that protected hundreds of Taliban soldiers, including Osama bin Laden. U.S. commanders wanted to pursue and neutralize bin Laden in an attempt to force an early demise to the global Al Qaeda network. A multidisciplinary team of roughly one hundred special operators from the Green Berets, Rangers, CIA special operations, and combat controllers was sent in to assist the local resistance fighters in capturing Tora Bora.

Tora Bora is a very rugged region with steep, rocky mountains and cliffs. Taliban fighters were deeply entrenched in their high-ground defensive positions, making it nearly impossible for ground forces to hike into reach of the cave system. Rather than foolishly risk the lives of U.S. or resistance fighters, the commanders of the U.S. ground forces decided to allow the assigned combat controller to deliver coordinated air strikes on Taliban positions.

Combat controller Tech Sergeant Michael Stockdale moved ahead of the U.S. forces forward defensive position and exposed himself to heavy fire from machine gun placements and mortar fire. TSgt. Stockdale used his BOA kit to call in precision attacks on Tora Bora fourteen hours a day, between

Combat controller airstrikes are visible for many miles and send a stern warning to the enemy.

December 6 and December 20, 2001. He called in precision bomb strikes, artillery, and AC-130 fire runs, and directed the dropping of the brutally devastating daisy cutter bomb.

Because of his efforts, TSgt. Stockdale was able to neutralize the majority of the Taliban forces in the Tora Bora cave network. His bravery under fire not only accomplished the mission of defeating the Taliban forces, but it saved the lives of countless U.S. and resistance fighters who surely would have perished trying to capture Tora Bora on foot. For his bravery and effort TSgt. Stockdale was awarded the Silver Star.

Combat controllers like Sgt. Stockdale are able to call in a wide variety of aircraft assaults and munitions types based on the conditions they see on the ground and on their assessment of what force needs to be applied. Using the Battlefield Operation Airman kit, the controller is able to view and update maps that are shared with the pilots and crews of aircraft. By highlighting enemy positions on the BAO kit, the pilots in air receive updates on their own maps, which helps them better navigate and aim their weaponry.

The firepower that a combat controller can wield is nearly unrivalled. The power of some of the heavier munitions that a controller can call for delivery is deadly in the extreme. This power comes with great responsibility because a mistake can take the lives of friendly forces. Even worse, it can take the lives of civilians. The controller has to take great care to be accurate when calculating attack calls and must verify that his targets are the enemy.

In the case of Tora Bora, a large portion of the enemy was clearly distinct from friendly forces because of their entrenched positions inside of the mountainside cave network. However, there were some enemies who had lower positions nearby the U.S. ODA (Operational Detachment Alpha) team, making it critical for TSgt. Stockdale to visibly identify and verify the enemy positions. The fog of war can make it easy for friendly forces to mistake one another for the enemy. If a controller were to call in an errant attack run on a friendly position, it could have a devastating effect. Therefore, the controller must take extra care to verify his targets.

BRAVERY UNDER FIRE

In 2006, in an undisclosed location in Afghanistan, combat controller TSgt. Scott Innis was deployed with a Special Forces team in a forward location deep in one of the many combat zones throughout the country. The team had taken station inside of a moderately defensible base with limited protection from enemy fire. During a routine patrol of the base perimeter, members of the ODA came under fire from an advancing enemy force with the intention of storming and eliminating the entire American presence.

TSgt. Innis used his skills and training to call in a close air support attack on the advancing enemy to help the American patrol team get back inside the relative safety of the base. Once the patrol team was back inside the perimeter, TSgt. Innis raced up to the top of a wooden observation tower in the center of the American base in order to gain a better vantage point to view the enemy and to call in air strikes against them.

Shortly after reaching the top of the tower, the base came under heavy fire from rocket-propelled grenades, mortars, and other artillery. TSgt. Innis received heavy small-arms fire on his position, and at great peril to his life he exposed himself to gain visibility of enemy positions. He called in air strikes, and during the moments of calm after each strike he would repeatedly expose himself to reestablish battlefield awareness of enemy positions to call in more air strikes. TSgt. Innis maintained his perilous position for twenty-four hours and called in constant air strikes throughout the entire engagement.

In addition to calling in air strikes, TSgt. Innis also called in and successfully guided multiple medical evacuation airlifts via helicopter. His efforts saved the lives of many of his teammates and protected the important forward base that American forces needed to maintain their ground presence in that region of Afghanistan.

DECORATED COMBAT CONTROLLERS

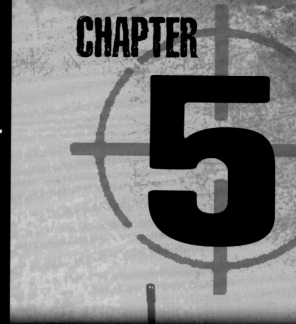

JANUARY, 2008: BARI KOWT, Afghanistan—Sgt. Robert Gutierrez was assigned to an ODA (Operational Detachment Alpha) that had joined forces with a team of Afghan border police to perform reconnaissance of the mountainous region around Bari Kowt, searching for a high-value Taliban target. The mission was intended to be a routine reconnaissance mission and was not intended for any substantial encounter with enemy forces.

While approaching the outskirts of Bari Kowt in the cover of darkness, the ODA team was ambushed by entrenched fighters in the town and the surrounding hills and cliffs. The enemy had high-powered machine guns, rocket-propelled grenades, mortars, and vastly superior numbers. Even though the ODA team was one of the best in the field, it quickly became apparent that they were in trouble.

Staff Sgt. Robert Gutierrez is one of the most highly decorated air force personnel. His awards include the Air Force Cross.

Within a few minutes of the ambush, the ODA captain was shot in the neck, and Green Berets Staff Sgt. Robert Miller, who was alongside Sgt. Gutierrez, ran to his side to attempt to save him. Shortly after making this move, Sgt. Miller was mortally wounded by a bullet shot to his chest and heart. As a trained special operations soldier, Gutierrez was unable to leave his fallen comrades to the enemy and remained alongside the bodies in an attempt to carry them out of the battle.

HUMANITARIAN EFFORTS OF THE CCT: HAITI

Following the devastating magnitude-8.0 earthquake that crippled Haiti in 2010, the U.S. Air Force sent teams of combat controllers to assist with the reactivation of the main airport at Port-au-Prince. Combat controllers were dropped into the area and then navigated on foot to the airport and took control of the air traffic tower. Over the course of several weeks, combat controllers operated as air traffic controllers, navigating hundreds of incoming and outgoing flights. At one point there was a flight landing or leaving every five minutes for twenty-four straight hours. The work of the Combat Control Team allowed the delivery of hundreds of thousands of pounds of relief material and equipment, and personnel.

Multiple enemy forces began converging on Sgt. Gutierrez's position, and he expertly eliminated many of the threats using his rifle and sidearm. The rest of his ODA team and the Afghan border patrol were several hundred yards behind Gutierrez's position, so he made the selfless decision to call in "Danger Close" firing runs from two A-10 Thunderbolts. He repeated this call more than a dozen times, and each time he was left unharmed while the enemy fighters around him were substantially reduced.

With not much choice left, Sgt. Gutierrez decided that he would have to retreat to a safer position, call in a substantial bombing run, and then return to gather the bodies of his fellow ODA members. He was able to distance himself to a less-than-ideal position and called in the bombing run, guiding the delivery of a 500-pound (227 kg) bomb on the nearby enemy positions. For his bravery under fire and selfless decision to call Danger Close air assaults on his own position, Sgt. Gutierrez was awarded the Bronze Heart with the "V" device for valor.

STAFF SGT. ZACHARY RHYNER: APRIL 2008, SHOK VALLEY, AFGHANISTAN

Sgt. Zachary Rhyner was attached to ODA 3336 on a mission to the Shok Valley in Afghanistan to engage with enemy forces known as the HIG that had aligned with the Taliban. The HIG were located in a small mountain village in the Shok Valley, which was 10,000 feet (3,048 meters) above sea level and accessible only by foot. ODA 3336 was divided into three units for the ascent up to the HIG-held village in order to minimize the risk from incoming enemy fire.

After a very challenging climb lasting several hours, the ODA was spotted by the entrenched pro-Taliban fighters. The pro-Taliban fighters immediately fired upon the ODA with heavy machine guns, RPGs, mortars, and sniper fire. The enemy forces had been living in this particular village for generations and had sophisticated defensive positions, making a counteroffensive nearly impossible.

Staff Sgt. Zachary Rhyner was awarded the Air Force Cross for his actions in Shok Valley, Afghanistan, in 2008.

45

In the very first moments of the ambush, several members of the ODA team were critically and mortally wounded, and Sgt. Rhyner was shot clean through the leg. The efforts of the ODA forward team to extract the dead and wounded were limited by the relentless enemy fire from above. Realizing that their situation was dire, the ODA commander issued orders to Sgt. Rhyner to call in air support to take out some of their attackers. Sgt. Rhyner called in a Danger Close assault that brought several missiles almost directly onto their location, but which did kill several enemy fighters.

Over the course of the next seven hours, Sgt. Rhyner called in seventy Danger Close air-to-ground assaults, including missile strikes, bomb drops, and the delivery of one 2,000-pound (907 kg) bomb that caused massive harm to the enemy forces.

Also assigned to that ODA team was Sgt. Gutierrez, a fellow combat controller and the highly decorated veteran of the Afghan war. The ODA was split into two strike teams to make the approach to the enemy positions redundant. Once shooting began, Sgt. Gutierrez was cut off from his fellow controller teammate by enemy fire and a fast-moving river between them. Over the course of several hours Sgt. Gutierrez and Sgt. Rhyner maintained radio communications to coordinate both helicopter and airplane movement in the area. After several hours of tracking and dodging bullets Sgt. Gutierrez was able to link with Sgt. Rhyner, and together they were able to better coordinate the efforts of the available air support to deliver precise ground support and munitions drops.

Throughout the seven-hour fight, Sgt. Rhyner endured the pain of his gunshot wound and never waivered in his duty to provide air support. When the enemy forces had been reduced by forty killed in action and one hundred wounded, an opening appeared for ODA 3336 to move to a safer extraction point for air evacuation.

Despite the alleviation of enemy gunfire upon their position, ODA 3336 still had to descend the rocky cliffs they had initially climbed. Their descent was made challenging by their efforts to lower wounded teammates down the cliffs while remaining hidden

AIR FORCE SILVER STAR

While attached to an army ODA, TSgt. Ismael Villegas and his team were clearing a road of explosive devices in September 2009 when they were suddenly ambushed by enemies with superior firing positions. Sgt. Villegas made a full dash through the mine field that his team had not yet completed removing, risking his life, to gain a better position from which to return fire and call in air support. Over the course of sixteen hours, Sgt. Villegas called in multiple air strikes from jets, helicopters, and artillery, saving the lives of his entire team. For his bravery and valor he was awarded one of the top honors bestowed by the U.S. Air Force.

from enemy firing positions. This was a treacherous movement even without the threat of enemy fire, and because of the nature of the terrain it was absolutely critical for Sgt. Rhyner to keep air support pressing upon the enemy forces to keep them from gaining any ground on the descending ODA.

THE FUTURE OF THE COMBAT CONTROL TEAM

Although the U.S. Air Force is the youngest of the armed services, its role has forever been cemented as a critical one. Ground commandos such as the Combat Control Team have become indispensible in warfare. Combat controllers make special operations teams more effective and represent the further integration of ground and air assault into one joint presence.

As more drone aircraft are put into service, it is critical that combat controllers be present to provide ground-based spotting and verification of targets to prevent unintended harm to noncombatants. Drones will also enable combat controllers to gain new access to information about the battlefield that was previously unavailable because they can go into situations that no pilot would dare.

Combat controllers are currently deploying with backpack-sized drone aircraft that they can carry with them into the field. These small drones give the combat controller new capabilities to peer into enemy territory with minimal observational risk. This information will certainly aid in the ability of the combat controller to deliver accurate information to both ground and air forces, thus saving lives and preserving equipment and valuable aircraft.

Further advancements in communications equipment will only enhance the battlefield awareness of combat controllers. Targeting systems, mapping tools, GPS systems, and other technological advancements will enable the controller to see parts of the battlefield that were previously invisible. This new awareness will allow the controller to deliver air attacks with more precision and with greater efficacy.

In order to make this future vision a reality, the AFSOC has created a special team of researchers and veteran CCT members to work with other branches of the military and civilian companies to find and test new cutting-edge equipment. This team studies new radio equipment, computer equipment, imaging systems, combat apparel, and weaponry. Once new equipment is developed and considered for use, it has to go through rigorous testing and refinement to ensure that it meets the rugged requirements of the CCT.

Some examples of the new equipment that combat controllers have begun adopting in field deployment are the SCAR-H assault rifle and newer lightweight body armor. The SCAR-H has been put into field service only since 2004. Prior to that, the M-4 had been the standard issue rifle. The SCAR-H provides enhanced durability, easier maintenance, and enhanced capabilities. Newer lightweight body armor provides enhanced protection of major body parts, and because of its lower weight it allows for more coverage of previously unprotected areas of the body.

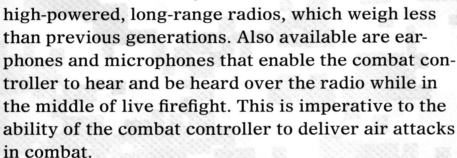

> *The combat controller emblem communicates what the team is all about: being "First There."*

The more of the body that can be armored, the more likely the soldier is to survive small-arms fire or explosive blast.

Advances in miniaturization have enabled combat controllers to carry high-powered, long-range radios, which weigh less than previous generations. Also available are earphones and microphones that enable the combat controller to hear and be heard over the radio while in the middle of live firefight. This is imperative to the ability of the combat controller to deliver air attacks in combat.

To continue to provide the air superiority that the special operations teams across the armed forces have come to depend upon, the AFSOC has increased its pipeline of combat control trainees. The CCT is going to grow substantially during the next decade in order to embed all special operations teams with combat controllers. The Combat Control Team is going to become a larger force with a global presence to deliver both combat operations support and further humanitarian relief efforts. To this effort, the AFSOC has begun to deploy veteran combat controllers throughout the United States on recruitment tours to educate prospective applicants about the CCT and to prequalify those candidates who seem to possess the physical and mental aptitude for the CCT. This prequalification enables the AFSOC to have a more robust pipeline of candidates who have the potential to successfully undergo CCT training.

In addition to developing new capabilities and resources for CCT use, the AFSOC has also begun to develop additional joint resource training opportunities for forward air controllers from other nations to learn from the success of the CCT. Prince Harry, the second son of Prince Charles of Wales, trained and fought alongside U.S. combat controllers in Afghanistan in 2008 during a joint training exercise between U.S. and British special operations.

Combat controllers represent the height of cross-disciplinary capabilities in the modern theater of war. As the nature of war continues to evolve, the allies of the United States will need to develop their own versions of the combat controller—a combination of commando, air technician, battlefield medic, and "eye in the sky." However, no matter the advances in equipment and training, one fact will remain true of the Combat Control Team—they will always be "First There."

GLOSSARY

AC-130 A four-engine, large aircraft in the U.S. Air Force fleet. Its purpose is to deliver massive and effective air-to-ground fire for the destruction of enemy combatants. Most commonly the AC-130 will work in coordination with a ground-based JTAC and will perform high-precision fire to neutralize enemy forces with minimal collateral damage.

AIR FORCE SPECIAL OPERATIONS COMMAND (AFSOC) A division of the U.S. Air Force that is designated for special operations. The AFSOC is the home of the Combat Control Team, along with several other commando units, and the home of the elite pilots who fly the AC-130, the PAVE-Hawk and PAVE-low helicopter, and the EC-130 fleet that delivers special operations teams around the world.

ARMY GREEN BERETS The most elite special operations group in the U.S. Army. The term "Special Forces" refers specifically to the Green Berets. They are trained in advanced combat, counterinsurgency, intelligence, languages, and retraining other forces. One of their key roles is providing training to friendly forces in support of the U.S. mission.

ARMY RANGERS A special operations force in the U.S. Army. They are highly trained combatants who specialize in ground warfare. Rangers have served in every combat operation since their inception. Army Rangers are highly skilled special tactics combatants.

CCUBA Acronym for "closed-circuit underwater breathing apparatus," the system and techniques used by underwater divers to re-breathe their own breath, with injections of oxygen, allowing them to swim submerged for extended periods of time, with no bubbles created by the device. This system enhances the diver's chance of going undetected while approaching hostile forces.

JOINT TERMINAL ATTACK CONTROLLER (JTAC) A designation assigned to any ground-based soldier who is trained to utilize the air-ground command and control network employed by the U.S. armed forces. JTACs are individuals who have trained and qualified to call in air strikes and evacuations and command airspace. All combat controllers are JTACs.

MARINE FORCE RECON ELITE Special operations group in the U.S. Marines. The key role of Force Recon is long-range, extended-duration reconnaissance of enemy positions well behind enemy lines. Force Recon units operate for weeks on end in the field without reinforcements. They are experts at covert movement, evasion, and intelligence gathering.

NAVY SEALS ELITE Special operations group in the U.S. Navy. The name comes from members' ability to operate in the sea, air, and land. SEALs are considered by many to be the most elite fighting force in the U.S. military.

OPERATIONAL DETACHMENT ALPHA (ODA) The name given to a U.S. Army Green Berets "A-Team." ODAs are typically comprised of ten Green Berets and one or two combat controllers.

PARARESCUE JUMPER (PJ) Elite combat rescue medics that serve in the U.S. Air Force. Their training is similar to that of the combat controller except that their advanced training focuses on paramedic skills.

PAVE A helicopter in the AFSOC fleet that is used by many special operations teams for delivery and extraction. It is a very large helicopter with extensive electronic equipment to allow it to travel very fast at low altitude in pitch dark to provide maximum covert advantage for its special operations payload.

PHYSICAL ABILITY AND STAMINA TEST (PAST) The physical fitness test administered by the AFSOC to determine if an Air Force CCT candidate is fit to meet the requirements of combat controller training.

SCUBA Acronym for "self-contained underwater breathing apparatus," the system and techniques used by underwater divers to breath from tanks of compressed air, allowing them to swim submerged for extended periods of time.

SPECIAL OPERATIONS COMMAND

(SOCOM) The operational group that overseas the activities of all special operations groups deployed across the entire U.S. armed forces.

SPECIAL OPERATIONS WEATHER (SOW)

A unit in the AFSOC that trains similarly to the CCT. However, SOWs are trained to provide combat weather forecasting, and their capabilities are invaluable to all of the armed forces. The SOWs' weather analytics can change entire battle plans and improve the effectiveness of U.S. forces.

SURVIVAL, EVASION, RESISTANCE, ESCAPE (SERE)

A type of training that prepares special operations commandos to deal with surviving in hostile territories. It covers survival in the wilderness and exposes trainees to simulated interrogation and torture. Special operations commandos must be prepared because they are very likely to be captured in their line of work.

TACTICAL AIR CONTROL PARTY (TACP)

Similar to combat controllers but not deployed with special operations teams in the same fashion. There are JTACs assigned to standard ground force units.

USA SPECIAL OPERATIONS COMMAND

(USASOC) USASOC is the command structure that encompasses the activities of SOCOM and all special operations teams across the entire U.S. armed forces.

FOR MORE INFORMATION

Special Forces Organization
4990 Doc Bennett Road
Fayetteville, NC 28306
(910) 485-5433
Web site: http://www.specialforcesassociation.org
According to the mission statement of the organization, "The Special Forces Association Serves as the Voice for the Special Forces Community; Perpetuates Special Forces Traditions and Brotherhood; Advances the Public Image of Special Forces and Promotes the General Welfare of the Special Forces Community."

The Special Operations Warrior Foundation
4409 El Prado Boulevard
Tampa, FL 33629
(877) 337-7693
Web site: http://www.specialops.org
The Special Operations Warrior Foundation provides full scholarship grants and educational and family counseling to the surviving children of special operations personnel who die in operational or training missions and immediate financial assistance to severely wounded special operations personnel and their families.

United States Special Operations Command
Headquarters, United States Special Operations Command
7701 Tampa Point Boulevard

MacDill Air Force Base, FL 33621

(813) 826-4600

Web site: http://www.socom.mil

This is the command center of the Special Operations
Command (SOCOM).

Veterans Affairs Canada

P.O. Box 7700

Charlottetown, PE C1A 8M9

Canada

(888) 996-2242

Web site: http://www.veterans.gc.ca/eng

This is the Canadian affairs office for military veterans.

WEB SITES

Due to the changing nature of Internet links, Rosen Publishing has developed an online list of Web sites related
to the subject of this book. This site is updated regularly.
Please use this link to access the list:

http://www.rosenlinks.com/ISF/CCT

FOR FURTHER READING

Blehm, Eric. *The Only Thing Worth Dying For: How Eleven Green Berets Forged a New Afghanistan.* New York, NY: Harper, 2010.

Cawthorne, Nigel. *Warrior Elite—31 Heroic Special-Ops Missions from the Raid on Son Tay to the Killing of Osama bin Laden.* Berkeley, CA: Ulysses Press, 2011.

Couch, Dick. *Chosen Soldier: The Making of a Special Forces Warrior.* New York, NY: Three Rivers Press, 2008.

Department of the Army. *U.S. Army Special Forces Handbook.* New York, NY: Skyhorse Publishing, 2008.

Fredriksen, John C. *Fighting Elites: A History of U.S. Special Forces.* Santa Barbara, CA: ABC: CLIO, 2012.

Friedrick, Jim. *TIME Special Ops: The Hidden World of America's Toughest Warriors.* New York, NY: TimeLife Books, 2011.

Guardia, Mike. *Shadow Commander: The Epic Story of Donald D. Blackburn: Guerrilla Leader and Special Forces Hero.* Havertown, PA: Casemate, 2011.

Maylor, Rob, with Robert Macklin. *Sniper Elite: The World of a Top Special Forces Marksman.* New York, NY: St. Martins, 2011.

McCullough, Jay, ed. *Ultimate Guide to U.S. Special Forces Skills, Tactics, and Techniques*. New York, NY: Skyhorse Publishing, 2011.

Robinson, Linda. *Masters of Chaos—The Secret History of the Special Forces*. New York, NY: Public Affairs-Perseus Books Group, 2005.

Tucker, David, and Christopher J. Lamb. *United States Special Operations Forces*. New York, NY: Columbia University Press, 2007.

Urban, Mark. *Task Force Black: The Explosive True Story of the Secret Special Forces War in Iraq*. New York, NY: St. Martin's Press, 2010.

BIBLIOGRAPHY

Adcock, Gene. *CCT @ the Eye of the Storm*. Fayetteville, NC: Combat Control School Heritage Foundation, 2009.

Call, Steve. *Danger Close: Tactical Air Controllers
in Afghanistan and Iraq*. Texas A&M University
Press: College Station, TX, 2007.

Carney, John T., and Benjamin F. Schemmer. *No
Room for Error—The Covert Operations of America's Special Tactics Units from Iran to Afghanistan*. New York, NY: Ballantine Books, 2002.

Cerasini, Mark. *The Complete Idiot's Guide to the
U.S. Special Forces*. Indianapolis, IN: Pearson
Education, 2002.

Lambeth, Benjamin S. *Air Power Against Terror:
America's Conduct of Operation Enduring Freedom*. Arlington, VA: RAND Corporation, 2006.

MacPherson, Malcolm. *Roberts Ridge*. New York, NY:
Bantam Dell, 2006.

Norrad, Wayne. U.S. Air Force Combat Controller,
retired, Public Relations Representative US Air
Force 720th Special Tactics Group. Interview:
April 5, 2012.

North, Oliver. *American Heroes in Special Operations*. Nashville, TN: Fidelis Publishing, 2010.

Pirnie, Bruce R., Alan J. Vick, Adam Grissom, Karl P.
Mueller, and David T. Orletzky. *Beyond Close Air*

Support: Forging a New Air-Ground Partnership. Arlington, VA: RAND Corporation, 2005.

Pushies, Fred. *Deadly Blue: Battle Stories of the U.S. Air Force Special Operations Command.* New York, NY: AMACOM Publishing, 2009.

Venturella, Paul. *Character, Competence and Commitment: The Measure of a Leader: Leadership Philosophies, Principles and Observations of a Career Air Force Combat Controller.* Bloomington, IN: AuthorHouse, 2007.

INDEX

ABOUT THE AUTHOR

Peter Ryan is an author of young adult reference books and an avid student of military history. He has a bachelor's degree in political science from Villanova University and an MBA from Rensselaer Polytechnic Institute.

PHOTO CREDITS

Cover inset and all interior photos courtesy of U.S. Air Force except: cover (flare) © iStockphoto.com/Evgeny Terentev; cover (smoke) © iStockphoto.com/Antagain; cover and interior (crosshairs) © iStockphoto.com/ marlanu; pp. 4, 7, 14, 22, 31, 41, 52, 56, 58, 60, 62 (spot texture) © iStockphoto.com/gary milner; pp. 7, 14, 22, 31, 41 (silhouette) © iStockphoto.com/Oleg Zabielin; p. 26 (bottom) courtesy AeroVironment, Inc., avinc .com; p. 32 © iStockphoto.com/Dvougao; p. 37 Romeo Gacad/AFP/Getty Images; interior background (camouflage) © iStockphoto.com/P_Wei.

Designer: Brian Garvey; Editor: Nicholas Croce; Photo Researcher: Marty Levick